To the one who adds color to my life, my husband, Myles

−S.L.P.

To my brother Scott and his family: Kim, Victoria, Rian, and Mason James.
I love you all

−M.C.P.

The Pinkneys gratefully acknowledge the participation of all the children photographed
for this book and salute the rainbow of ethnic groups they represent: Yellow - African
American; Blue - Hungarian/Italian; Red - Pakistani; Orange - Mexican/Aztec/Italian;
Purple - Taiwanese; Black - Jordanian; Green - African American/Native
American/Portuguese; Pink - Dutch/German; Brown - Vietnamese;
White - El Salvadoran; Tan - West African. The rainbow painters are African
American, Indian, Puerto Rican/Mexican, and British/Austrian. Many thanks to all.

Text copyright © 2002 by Sandra L. Pinkney.
Photographs copyright © 2002 by Myles C. Pinkney.
All rights reserved. Published by Scholastic Inc.
SCHOLASTIC, CARTWHEEL BOOKS, and associated logos are trademarks and/or
registered trademarks of Scholastic Inc.

Library of Congress Cataloging-in-Publication Data

Pinkney, Sandra L.
A rainbow all around me / by Sandra L. Pinkney ; photographs by Myles C. Pinkney. p.   cm.

ISBN 0-439-30928-X

[1. Color— Fiction. 2. Rainbow—Fiction.] I. Pinkey, Myles C. II. Title.
PZ7.P63348 Rai 2002 [E]—dc21 2001040017

10 9 8 7 6 5 4 3 2 1   02 03 04 05 06

Printed in Mexico 49
First printing, February 2002

A RAINBOW *All Around Me*

by Sandra L. Pinkney ✱ Photographs by Myles C. Pinkney

Cartwheel
·B·O·O·K·S· ®

SCHOLASTIC INC.

New York Toronto London Auckland Sydney Mexico City New Delhi Hong Kong Buenos Aires

Colors

are in everything I see.
A piece of the rainbow—
you and me.

YELLOW

Smiling faces

BRIGHT.

Fun

SUNSHINE in the RAIN

BLUE

Cool

RUGGED

Sippin' on a hot day
Relaxing in the **BREEZE**

RED

HOT

Full of LOVE

CINNAMONY sweet
A Happy **VALENTINE**

Colors *are you.*
Colors *are me.*

ORANGE

Fruity

Tangy

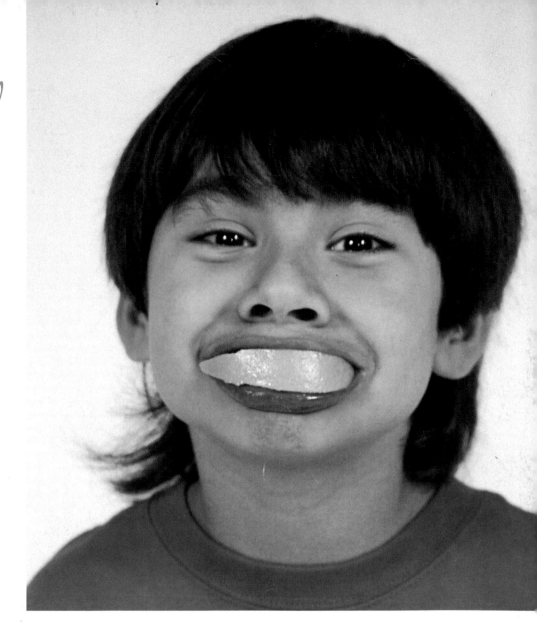

Poppin' in your mouth
BURSTING with **flavor**

PURPLE

WILD

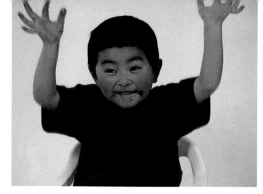

CrAzy

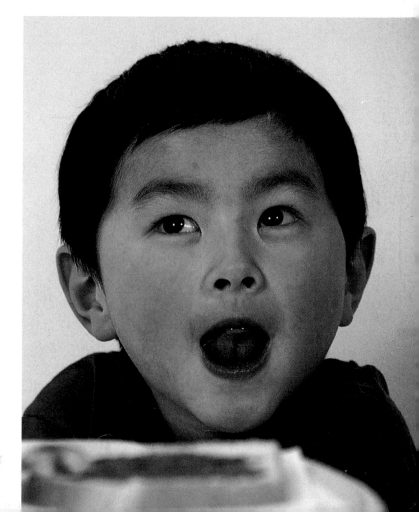

Nutritious and *delicious*
JAMMIN' on a slice of bread

BLACK

Tappin'

Rhythm

Moving feet
Dancin' to the **beat**

Colors *are you.*
Colors *are me.*

GREEN

Fresh

Soft blades

Ticklin' your TOES
Barefoot in the park

PINK

CHEWY

Gooey

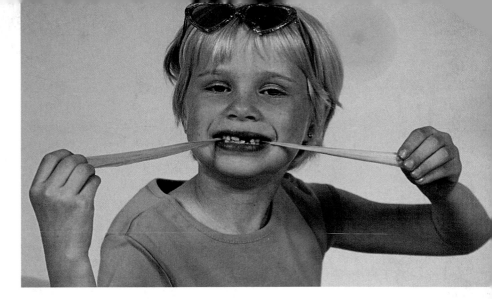

Bubblin' fun
Sticking to your face

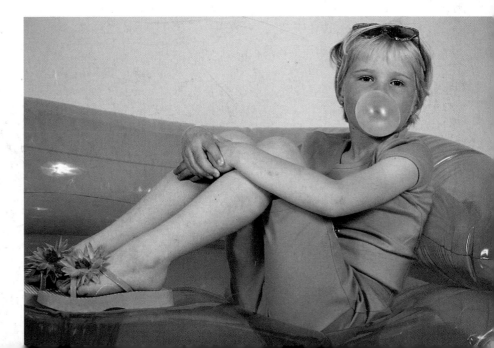

BROWN

Soft

Huggable

Comfort
through the night
My **BEST** friend

Colors *are you.*
Colors *are me.*

WHITE

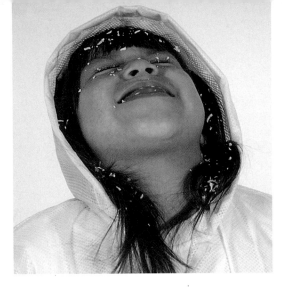

COLD

Crystalline

Falling from the sky
Meltin' on your TONGUE

TAN

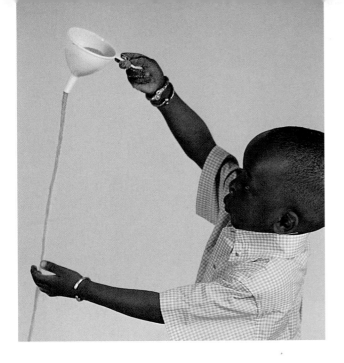

GRITTY

Itty-bitty rocks

Sparklin' in the SUNLIGHT
Castle made for a **KING**

Colors!
COLORS!
They're in *everything* I see!
We are the rainbow—
YOU and ME!